Contents

Life cycles

All living things have a life cycle.

guin's

e

kmann

ARIES

www.raintreepublishers.co.uk
Visit our website to find out
more information about
Raintree books.

To order:
☎ Phone 0845 6044371
📠 Fax +44 (0) 1865 312263
✉ Email myorders@raintreepublishers.co.uk

Customers from outside the UK please telephone +44 1865 312262

Raintree is an imprint of Capstone Global Library Limited,
a company incorporated in England and Wales having its
registered office at 7 Pilgrim Street, London, EC4V 6LB
– Registered company number: 6695582

Edited by Nancy Dickmann, Rebecca Rissman, and Catherine Veitch
Designed by Joanna Hinton-Malivoire
Picture research by Mica Brancic
Production by Victoria Fitzgerald
Originated by Capstone Global Library
Printed and bound in China by South China Printing Company Ltd

ISBN 978 0 431 00949 0 (hardback)
15 14 13 12 11
10 9 8 7 6 5 4 3 2 1

ISBN 978 0 431 00957 5 (paperback)
15 14 13 12 11
10 9 8 7 6 5 4 3 2 1

British Library Cataloguing in Publication Data
Dickmann, Nancy.
A penguin's life. -- (Watch it grow)
598.4'7156-dc22
A full catalogue record for this book is available from the British Library.

Acknowledgements
We would would like to thank the following for permission to reproduce
photographs: Ardea pp. 7 (Graham Robertson), 9 (Auscape); FLPA p. **16**
(Minden Pictures/Ingo Arndt); Nature Picture Library pp. 5 (© Fred Olivier),
21 (© David Tipling); Photolibrary pp. 4 (Flirt Collection/Kevin Dodge),
6 (Oxford Scientific Films (OSF)/Kjell Sandved), **8** (Oxford Scientific Films
(OSF)/David Tipling), **10** (Cusp/Frank Krahmer [Oxford Scientific Films
(OSF)/David Tipling]), **11** (Oxford Scientific Films (OSF)/Mike Tracey),
12 (Picture Press/Thorsten Milse), **13** (age fotostock/Morales Morales),
14 (Oxford Scientific Films (OSF)/Tui De Roy), **15** (Oxford Scientific Films
(OSF)/Tui De Roy), **17** (Oxford Scientific Films (OSF)/Doug Allan), **18**
(All Canada Photos/Wayne Lynch), **19** (Oxford Scientific Films (OSF)/
Doug Allan), **20** (Tsuneo Nakamura), **22 bottom** (Oxford Scientific Films
(OSF)/Tui De Roy), **22 left** (Oxford Scientific Films (OSF)/Tui De Roy),
22 right (Picture Press/Thorsten Milse), **22 top** (Oxford Scientific Films
(OSF)/David Tipling), **23 bottom** (Oxford Scientific Films (OSF)/Mike
Tracey), **23 middle bottom** (Picture Press/Thorsten Milse), **23 middle
top** (age fotostock/Morales Morales), **23 top** (Oxford Scientific Films
(OSF)/Tui De Roy).

Front cover photograph of emperor penguins in Antarctica reproduced with
permission of Corbis (© Paul Souders). Inset photograph of an emperor
penguin egg reproduced with permission of Photolibrary (Oxford Scientific
(OSF)/David Tipling). Back cover photograph of an emperor penguin with
an egg reproduced with permission of Ardea (Graham Robertson).

The publishers would like to thank Dee Reid, Diana Bentley, and
Nancy Harris for their assistance in the preparation of this book.

Every effort has been made to contact copyright holders of material
reproduced in this book. Any omissions will be rectified in subsequent
printings if notice is given to the publisher.

Penguins have a life cycle.

A chick hatches. It grows into a penguin.

egg

A penguin lays eggs. Later it will die.

Eggs

A female penguin lays an egg
in winter.

egg

She gives the egg to a male penguin.

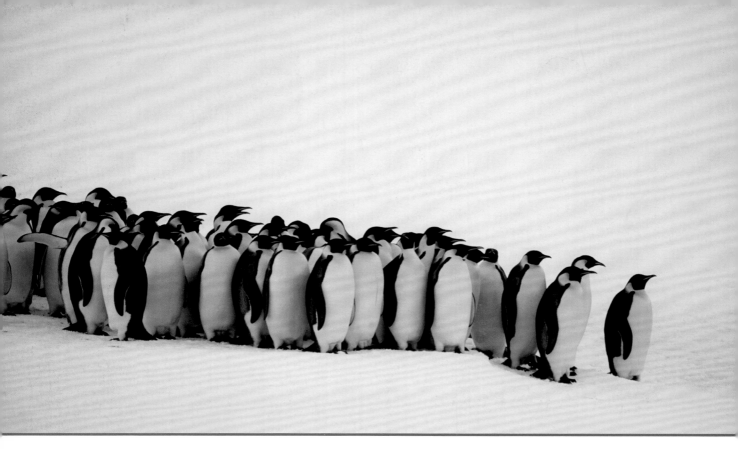

It is very cold in winter.

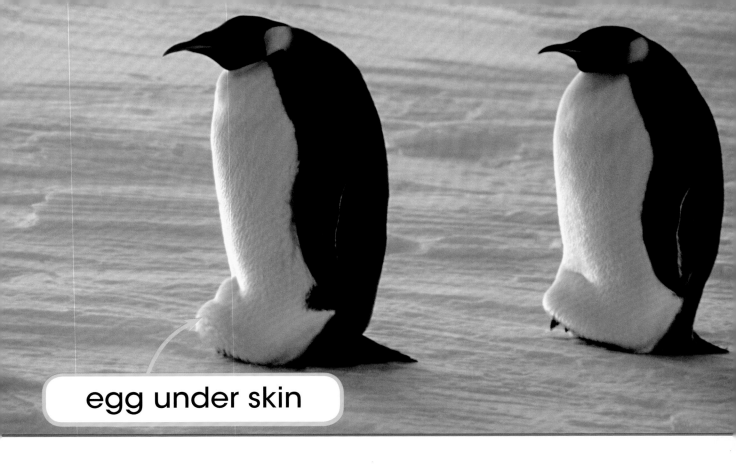

egg under skin

The male penguin keeps the egg
warm on his feet.

Chicks

A chick hatches from the egg.

Its parent gives it food.

The chick has fluffy grey feathers.
Soon they fall out.

There are white and black feathers under the grey ones.

Becoming a penguin

The young penguin learns to swim.

The young penguin catches fish
to eat.

The penguins walk across the ice
in autumn.

They meet up in a big group.

A female penguin lays an egg.

The life cycle starts again.

Life cycle of a penguin

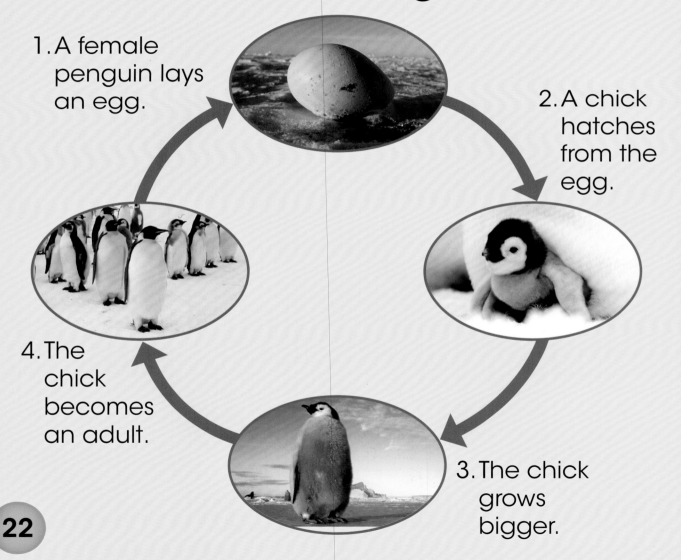

1. A female penguin lays an egg.

2. A chick hatches from the egg.

3. The chick grows bigger.

4. The chick becomes an adult.

22

Picture glossary

feather body covering on birds

female able to have babies. A girl is a female.

hatch to be born from an egg

male able to be a father. A boy is a male.

Index

Notes to parents and teachers

Before reading

Show the children a photo of a penguin's egg and ask them if they know what animal laid it. Give them a clue by showing them photos of Antarctica. Tell the children the animal that laid the egg lives in a very cold place. Show them photos of some of the animals that live in Antarctica, including a penguin. Can they guess now? What type of animal do they think a penguin is? Show them a photo of a chicken. Do they think a penguin is a bird? Tell the children that all birds lay eggs. Discuss the penguin's features that are similar to and different from a chicken.

After reading

• Show a clip from a wildlife programme of penguins in Antarctica, such as from BBC's Planet Earth. Talk about how cold Antarctica is and how the penguins keep their eggs and each other warm. Show the children the photographs on pages 11 and 19 in this book to help them understand.

• Make a list with the children of how they keep warm when they are outside on a cold day. Discuss what it would be like to live in a very cold place.

• In PE, give each child a beanbag to balance on their feet and pretend that they are a penguin balancing an egg on its feet. Is it easy? Can they walk with the beanbag on their feet?